Introduction

White Horse hill carvings are indigenous to Wiltshire. There are more here than anywhere else in the world, but of the thirteen that once stood on its grassy slopes only eight are still visible.

People are sometimes dismayed to discover that they are not as old as other well-known Wiltshire landmarks such as Avebury and Stonehenge. Most are antiquities of only a few hundred years yet their origins lie firmly in ancient times. The oldest white horse at Uffington is believed to be around 3,000 years old.

Although the Uffington horse is the oldest there may have been others that were not lucky enough to survive the rigours of nature over such a massive span of time.

Chalk is a fairly soft and friable type of rock made from compacted fossilised seashells

ox ... ere ... the centre pages.

Care should be taken not to leave any valuables in your vehicle when it is unattended.

Tour Directions

Use this box if you want to take the circular tour. The chapters are in order but you can start at whichever horse you like. It follows a roughly clockwise direction and the map on the centre pages will help you.

Cherhill Horse

that were laid down beneath the oceans at the time of dinosaurs. Britain has an unusually large amount of chalk within its shores. Geological forces pushed the chalk up to form the downlands that are characteristic of this area.

It was on these hills that ancient man developed this unique type of folk art. Where the turf naturally fell away it revealed the whiteness below that could be seen for miles around. Using this striking contrast to create pictures and landmarks was a natural progression. The horse was probably chosen because it had sacred status and symbolised strength and fertility. The shape worked well and the trend continued to the later horses. Although a few have appeared elsewhere in Britain for some reason it is Wiltshire where the art really captured the imagination.

Cutting a horse was a difficult task. As they were meant to be seen from the ground simply drawing a horse on a hill without adjusting the design to allow for the slope meant the horse looked distorted. This is called foreshortening. One way that creators overcame this problem was to stand some distance away and direct others to rearrange the outline until it looked right. Unfortunately in days before mobile phones and two-way radios this would have meant shouting loudly or trekking back and forth to relay the information.

Once the outline was marked out the turf was removed to expose the white rock behind. Sometimes the soil was deeper in certain areas or the chalk not very white so a method developed where the shape was dug to a uniform depth then filled and packed with clean chalk excavated from elsewhere on the hill. Weeds took longer to grow on this surface, and it also proved to be harder wearing against

Chalk exposed due to natural erosion

Hackpen Horse in need of scouring

the wind and rain.

As with their living counterparts they require regular grooming or scouring. Every few years the edges are tidied and the worn discoloured chalk replaced with fresh. The scouring of older horses was accompanied by festivities for the workers at the expense of the landowner. At Uffington this was known as the 'Pastime' and was reputed to have taken place every seven years although in practise it was a little less regular.

The news of these festivals may have helped the revival of hill carving in the 1700 and 1800s.

In 1949 Morris Marples coined the phrase 'leucippotomy' for the cutting of chalk hill figures.

After the Westbury horse was recut in 1778 it was not long before another appeared at Cherhill.

Although a horse should be scoured around every seven years to prevent it looking like an old grey mare some have been able to survive with as few as three scourings a century. Of course where outlines were overgrown certain areas would have been recut. The position of feet especially has been known to change over the years.

These days local people are usually very fond of their particular horse and feel quite strongly if it falls into disrepair. Almost all money for restoration is raised by charities formed to protect the horses. Local community groups and other volunteers often carry out the work ensuring the remaining horses will be with us for many years to come.

Westbury Horse

Westbury Horse

Also known as the Bratton Horse this is the largest, oldest and most interesting of the Wiltshire horses.

Situated on a very steep slope with the Iron Age hill fort called Bratton Camp above and the Pewsey Vale stretching out below it is perhaps not surprising that this perfect site was once home to another horse.

An air of mystery surrounds the earlier example as it is difficult to say with any certainty who was responsible for its creation.

It was a right facing stallion much smaller than the present mare but these were not the only differences. The first horse was rather strange in appearance with a large central eye, a saddlecloth and an upturned tail ending as a crescent. This finishing touch to the

Location

OS grid reference: ST 898 516

2 miles (3km) east of Westbury off B3098. On Bratton Down below the Iron Age hill fort called Bratton Castle overlooking the Vale of Pewsey.

Tour Directions

Distance 22 miles (35½ km)

From Alton Barnes horse continue to Devizes. Then take the A360 towards Salisbury. When you reach West Lavington turn right onto B3098. A viewing area is situated on the right after approximately 8 miles (13km). To visit the horse retrace to the village of Bratton and turn right into Castle Road. There is a free parking area on top of the hill and short footpath to the horse.

tail seems a strange addition until we see that the characteristics of the horse resemble the artwork on Iron Age coins (see page 23). A crescent moon is often seen above the rear of a horse on these coins and it is possible that there was one here too until, in a later scouring, it was thought to be the end of the tail and was mistakenly joined up.

With these similarities and the fact that it is situated below an Iron Age hill fort, like the horse at Uffington, it seems reasonable to suggest that it also dates from this time.

Early antiquarians thought that it was cut by King Alfred to celebrate the victory of the Battle of Ethandun (AD 878), which was supposed to have been fought in the area.

Yet some believe that it was made around 1700 as a fake or pseudo-antique, the building of temples and follies by rich landowners was becoming popular, although this theory is based on the account of one man. In 1742 he had spoken to the locals and was told that 'it had been wrought within the memory of persons now living or but lately

Fact File

Original horse of unknown date
Present horse cut in 1778
Oldest Wiltshire horse
Largest Wiltshire horse
55½ metres (182 ft) nose to tail
33 metres (108 ft) ear to hoof
Visible from 20 miles (32km)
Slope 45°
Best view from viewing area on B3098

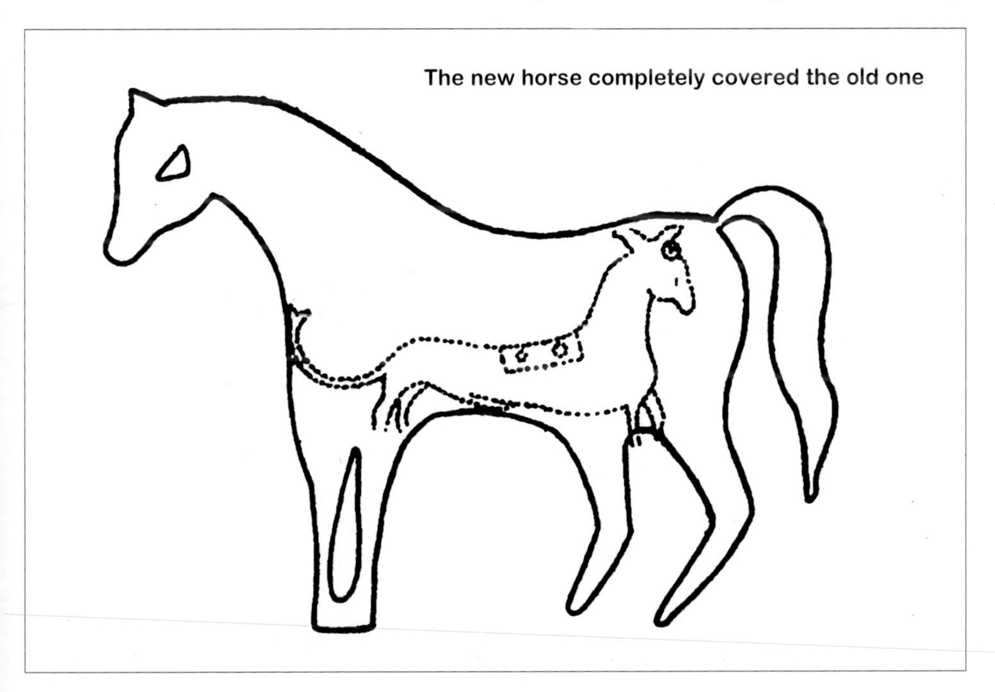
The new horse completely covered the old one

The Hind Legs

dead.' As we shall see with other accounts of white horses it is not a very reliable source, and it could just have been a recollection of a thorough scouring.

An appropriately named George Gee cut the new horse in 1778. Mr G Gee did not like the old horse and decided to redesign it in a more fashionable style. Stubbs had become a highly regarded painter of animals, in particular horses, and the new horse shows a definite likeness to some of his pictures.

As with all the later Wiltshire horses (except Devizes) he made it face left but because this was the first it obviously was not following a trend. For some reason if asked to draw a horse most people will draw it facing left. The new design was large enough that the old horse's outline did not need be taken into consideration.

A drawing of the old horse from Gough's edition of Camden's 'Britannia' set inside a drawing of the new horse by Plenderleath shows how, even when turned around, the new horse completely consumed it.

With the onset of the Second World War it became apparent that such a prominent landmark needed to be camouflaged from the sight of enemy aircraft. It was preserved by covering it first with roofing felt then with turf.

The Head

A figure on such a steep slope inevitably suffered with erosion. In the 1873 restoration edging stones were used to help keep the chalk in place and later drainage gratings were installed at the feet. Even though the problem was reduced it was not entirely overcome until in the 1950s when it was decided to cover the horse in concrete and paint the whole thing white. It was a sad decision but one taken to relieve the burden of intense maintenance and the costs it bore.

Perhaps it is fitting for the horse to have a coat of concrete because Westbury is home to a large cement works. Its constantly billowing chimney blights the view of the Pewsey Vale.

In the summer the strong updraft makes the hill top a popular place with kite flyers and paragliders. With good eyes in fair weather you may also be able to see the Cherhill and Alton Barnes horses from here.

Devizes Horse

Devizes Horse

Devizes white horse was created to celebrate the new millennium.

Many years ago there was a horse on Roundway down north of the town below the hill fort known as Oliver's Castle. This horse was cut by local shoemakers in 1845 at Witsun and was known as Snob's horse (dialect for shoemaker). It was a good site with a steep slope that would have made it visible from a great distance. But it was not maintained and by the end of the century had completely grown over. Occasionally though during a hot dry summer the outline could be discerned from a slight change in the colour of the grass where the horse once stood.

In 1954 a schoolboy named Peter Greed saw the outline and completed a detailed drawing of it.

Location

OS grid reference: SU 016 641

North of Devizes off A361. It lies on Roundway Hill overlooking Hopton Industrial Estate and Roundway village.

Tour Directions

Distance 14 miles (22½ km)

From the Westbury horse turn right onto B3098 and continue to West Lavington. At the crossroads turn left onto A360 to Devizes. From Devizes take the A361 towards Swindon. After almost a mile (1.5km) turn left signed Roundway. You will see the horse ahead. Turn right by the phone box and follow the road up the hill taking the right hand fork. Free parking is available above the horse.

He had an idea that one day he would like to recut the horse. It was not until Devizes was looking for a project to commemorate the millennium that his dream was realised.

The original site was unavailable as it was privately owned so a new site was chosen about 1mile (1.5km) to the east of the old horse. Peter Greed's drawing of the old horse was used only the ground favoured a mirrored image making it the only horse in Wiltshire to face right. Unfortunately in using the original shape on a slope that is not as steep the effect of foreshortening is all too apparent. No changes were made to the design to counter the effect.

The town was behind the project. Local businesses lent their support and around 200 local people turned out to help. The chalk was excavated from beneath the outline using heavy machinery and the eye was defined by a sarsen boulder. And, so there will be no doubt in future generations as to the dating of this horse, a time capsule containing items of the twentieth century with significance to Devizes and Britain was buried underneath the horse's head.

The new horse was finished in September 1999 in good time for the celebrations. The horse was bathed in light from dusk on the eve of the millennium until dawn on New Year's Day.

Fact File

Cut in 1999
Youngest Wiltshire horse
Only right facing horse in Wiltshire
Best view from Hopton Industrial Estate and Roundway village.

The Head

Cherhill Horse

Like the Westbury horse this fine example also lies on a steep 45° slope beneath an Iron Age hill fort called Oldbury Castle.

During the 1800s it was a landmark that passengers would look out for on the long carriage journey from Bath to London.

It was Calne resident Dr Christopher Alsop who created it in 1780. He was a keen amateur engineer but was known locally as the 'mad doctor' probably because he was mad enough to cut a white horse.

It was only two years after the Westbury horse was remodelled that Dr Alsop realised Cherhill's potential. The hillside was perfect to display a hill figure. So good in fact that one cannot help but wonder if there was ever an old horse here as well. The similarities

Location

OS grid reference: SU 049 696

4 miles (6½ km) east of Calne off A4. On Cherhill Down below hill fort called Oldbury Castle overlooking Cherhill village.

Tour Directions

Distance 8½ miles (13½ km)

From the Devizes horse turn left onto A361. After the dual carriageway take the next left towards Calne. After 3½ miles (5½ km) turn right at the T-junction onto the A4. The horse can be seen before you. To get to the horse you can park in one of the lay-bys at the bottom of the hill and walk up.

Cherhill Horse

The Head

between this and the sites of Uffington and Westbury cannot be ignored as all of them lie below hill forts. Unfortunately, despite the coincidences no evidence of an older horse has ever been found.

The new horse at Westbury must have been what inspired Dr Alsop. Its design was of the same type only it was a little smaller and walking rather than standing.

The ancient art of hill carving was beginning a revival.

Alsop's men pegged out the horse with small white flags while he himself shouted directions to them through a megaphone from below.

This explains why this horse looks so good from the ground. Using this method there are none of the effects of foreshortening that you see with some other horses.

The outline was excavated to about 15cm (6 inches) and packed with chalk from the other side of the hill. The eye, just over a metre (4 ft) across, was filled with upturned glass bottles, which gave it a unique and rather ingenious twinkle.

Over time the bottles disappeared probably to souvenir hunters. An attempt to return the glint to its eye was carried out in 1971 by local school children who

Fact File

Cut in 1780
Second largest Wiltshire horse
39 metres (129ft) nose to tail
43 metres (142ft) ear to hoof
Visible from 30 miles (48km)
Slope 45°
Best view is from the A4 Calne to Beckhampton road

Cherhill's walking pose

collected fifty bottles and positioned them to recreate the original effect. But unfortunately these too have now disappeared. The eye is now made from rather dull stones set in concrete.

Scouring has been carried out about every seven years by the successive landowners and more recently by local volunteers and community groups. But there seems to have been no incentives as in the case of the Uffington horse where the landowner laid on a festival to reward the workers. Instead local labour was given freely with the chalk still excavated from another part of the hill. The last major restoration work was carried out in 2002 with funds raised by the Cherhill White Horse Restoration Group.

'The horse was grey, but now is white,
It didn't happen overnight,
To keep it looking just as bright,
A pound from you will see us right.'

This poem was written to encourage visitors to make donations towards the horse's

Cherhill Down

upkeep and is displayed beside a secure collection box at the bottom of the hill.

There has always been a strong local attachment to this horse, which still continues today. That is not to say that it has always been treated with respect. It has been known for pranksters to change the sex of the horse and once it even changed species. One morning it was discovered that it had become a zebra! More recently it has been used in a car advertisement.

Lansdowne Column

Besides the white horse and Oldbury Castle there is another monument on the Downs that deserves a mention. The Lansdowne Column was built in 1845 by the third Marquis of Lansdowne in memory of his ancestor Sir William Petty (1623-1687). It was placed on this hill so it he could easily see it from his home at Bowood House.

Broad Town Horse

This trotting horse lies on the most western limit of the same escarpment that is home to the horse at Uffington and overlooks the far end of the Vale of the White Horse.

There are several different stories of the origin of this horse. The date most usually used is 1864 when the landowner of the time, William Simmonds, claimed he carved it. His initial design was for a fairly small horse as he intended to increase the size of the outline with each scouring. This would not have been a very effective way of enlarging the horse; the neck for example could not be made longer without moving the head. So perhaps it is just as well that he gave up the farm before he had chance to try his idea and we have been spared the sight of a very

Location

OS grid reference: SU 098 783

½ mile (800m) north-east of Broad Town.
Overlooks the village.

Tour Directions

Distance 11½ miles (18½ km)

From the Cherhill horse continue on the A4 until you reach the roundabout at Beckhampton. Take the first exit towards Avebury. After approximately 4 miles (6½ km) turn left to Broad Hinton and continue into the village of Broad Town. The horse can be seen on your right as you descend the hill. It is best to park in the village and walk from there.

Broad Town Horse

The Head

distorted figure with a short neck and thick legs!

Another story which would date the horse much earlier is from a former curator of the Imperial War Museum who claimed that as a boy, in about 1863, he and a friend had spent four or five hours scouring the horse. He was told by an elderly relative that the horse had already been there for at least fifty years. It is possible that he had confused it with another nearby horse.

Throughout the horse's history there have been several times when it was so overgrown it was almost invisible so it is not surprising that there is yet another version, though rather vague, of when it was cut.

Apparently a Mr Hussey, Horsley or even Horsey was supposed to have cut the horse in1896. This must have been a case of recutting after a spell of neglect.

During the Second World War it was successfully camouflaged with hedge trimmings covered with soil and turf. It reappeared again in 1945 although its condition was not good.

Thankfully in 1991, due to strong local opinion, a society was formed to take on responsibility for the horse's upkeep and since then it has been scoured regularly.

Fact File

Cut in 1864?
24½ metres (80ft) nose to tail
18 metres (58ft) ear to hoof
Visible from 20 miles (32km)
Slope 45°
Best view is from Broad Town village

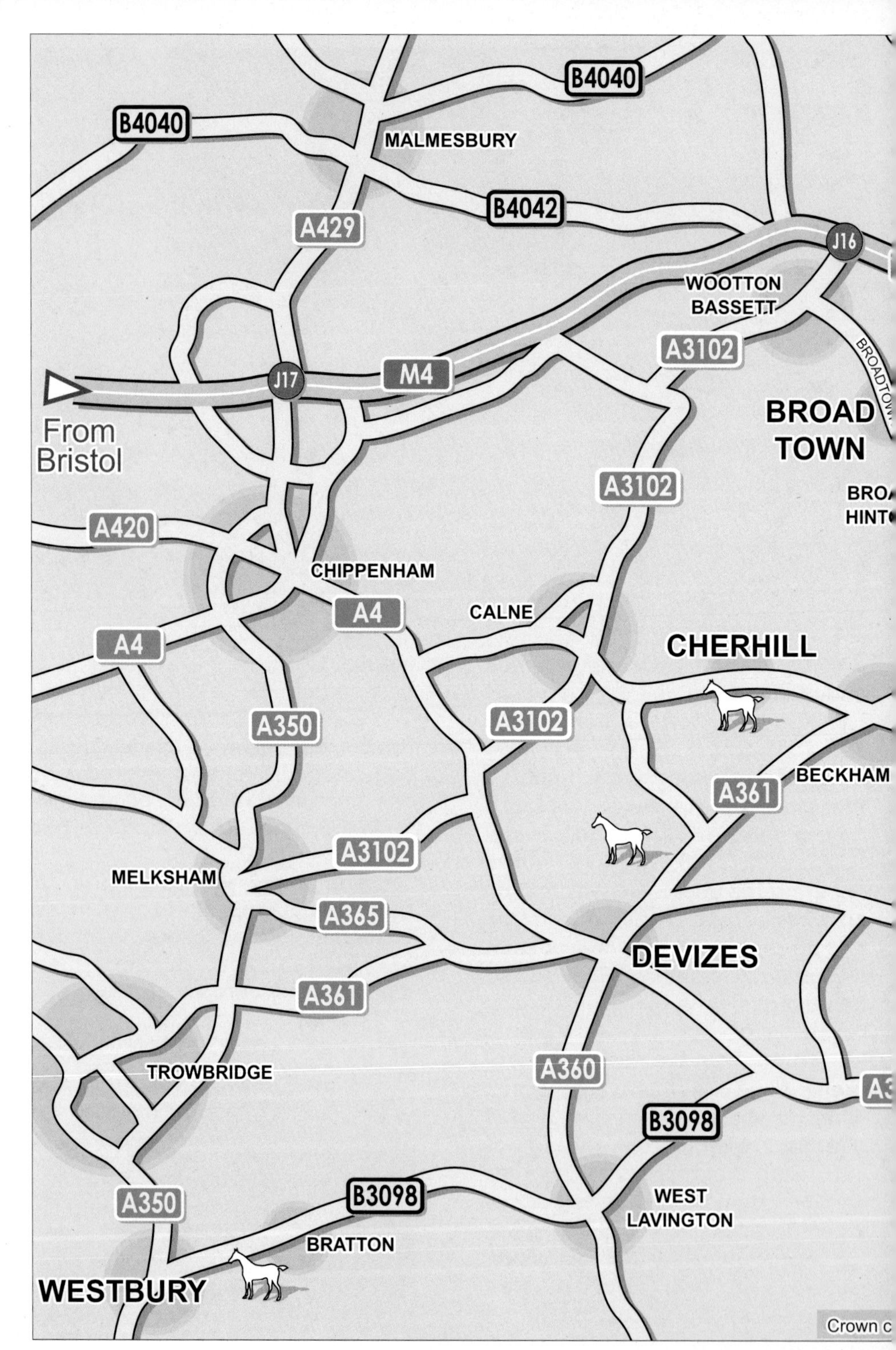
B4040
B4040
MALMESBURY
B4042
A429
J16
WOOTTON
BASSETT
A3102
BROADTOWN
From
Bristol
J17
M4
BROAD
TOWN
A3102
A420
CHIPPENHAM
A4
CALNE
A4
CHERHILL
A350
A3102
A361
BECKHAM
A3102
MELKSHAM
A365
DEVIZES
A361
TROWBRIDGE
A360
B3098
A350
B3098
WEST
LAVINGTON
BRATTON
WESTBURY

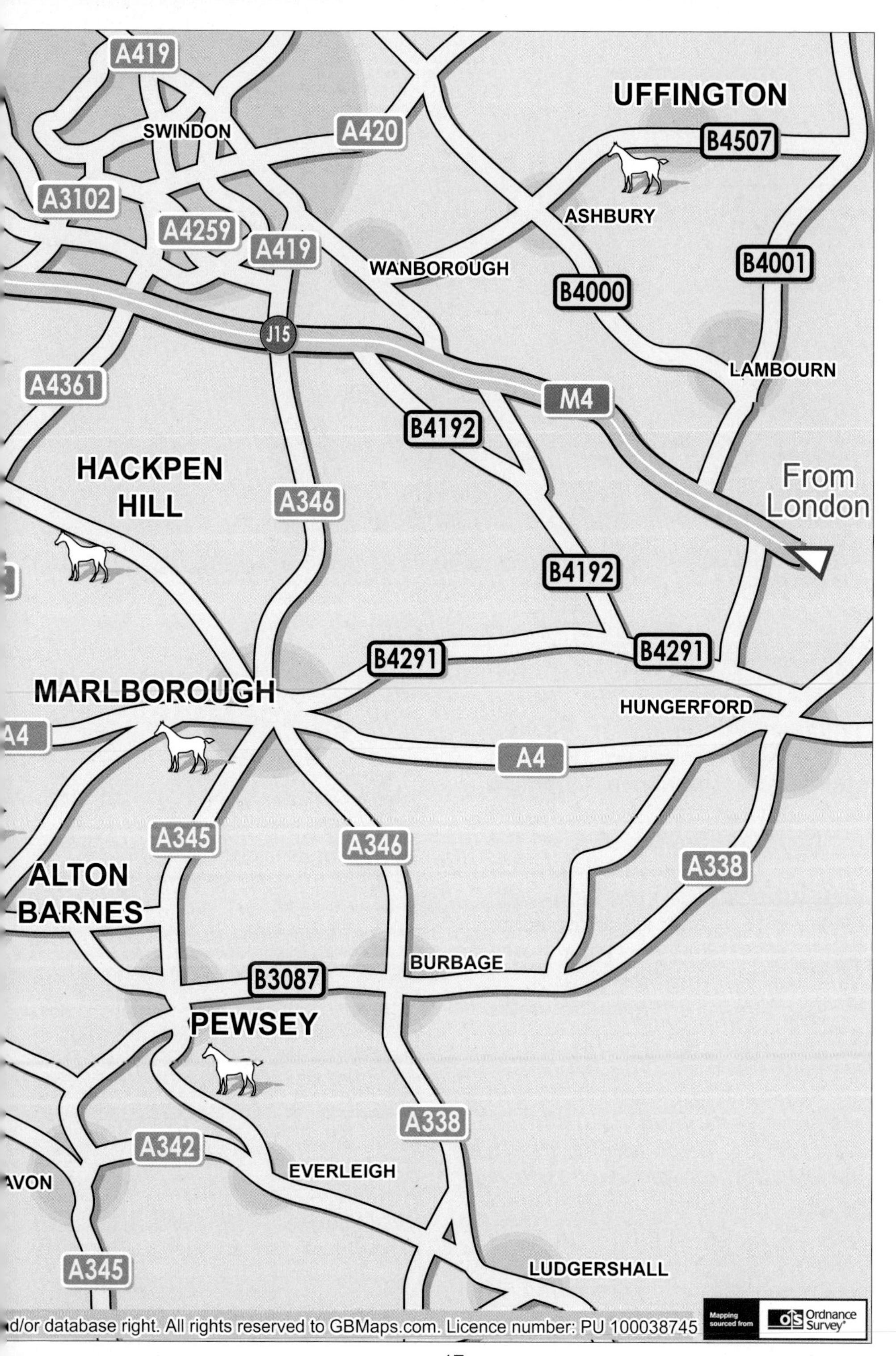
A419
UFFINGTON
SWINDON
A420
B4507
A3102
ASHBURY
A4259
A419
B4001
WANBOROUGH
B4000
J15
LAMBOURN
A4361
M4
B4192
HACKPEN
HILL
A346
From
London
B4192
B4291
B4291
MARLBOROUGH
HUNGERFORD
A4
A4
A345
A346
A338
ALTON
BARNES
BURBAGE
B3087
PEWSEY
A338
A342
EVERLEIGH
AVON
A345
LUDGERSHALL
Mapping sourced from
Ordnance Survey

Hackpen Horse

Hackpen Horse

Also known as the Broad Hinton or Winterbourne Bassett horse this horse can be seen trotting across Hackpen Hill, which forms the north-west limit of the Marlborough Downs. Above the horse on the top of the hill is the ancient track called the Ridgeway. It follows the chalk ridge for some 85 miles (137km) from Overton Hill, Wiltshire to Ivinghoe Beacon in Buckinghamshire. Fantastic views of the Wiltshire countryside can be had from here.

Not much is known about how this horse originated but generally the credit is given to the parish clerk of 1838. His name was Henry Eatwell and he was assisted in his task by a local publican. It is believed to have been done to commemorate the coronation of Queen Victoria.

Location

OS grid reference: SU 128 749

Lies off the A4361 on Hackpen Hill below The Ridgeway on the north-west limit of Marlborough Downs.

Tour Directions

Distance 4 miles (6½ km)

From Broad Town horse retrace your path back to the A4361 Avebury to Swindon Road. You can see the horse ahead as you approach the junction. Almost opposite is the road that leads to the horse. There is free parking above the horse where the Ridgeway Path crosses the road.

The horse is facing left and has a rather slender neck and legs making it look quite graceful. The best view is from the Avebury to Swindon road (A4361) because as you get nearer on the minor road it becomes frustratingly more difficult to see.

The slope is gentle being only 30° and to make up for the foreshortening effect the head and ears were banked up. But over time the rain washed chalk down to the feet banking these up in the opposite direction making the problem even worse!

The road curls around the horse and makes its way up to the brow of the hill. Where the Ridgeway crosses the road there is room to park a few cars.

The horse was camouflaged from enemy aircraft during World War II. When this was removed the horse was in good condition but regular scouring was not carried out and only occasional superficial tending stopped the horse from disappearing altogether.

When it is in good condition it can be seen from the downs near the Cherhill horse.

Fact File

Cut in 1838

27½ metres (90 feet) nose to tail

27½ metres (90 feet) ear to hoof

Visible from surrounding villages

Slope 30°

Best view is from the A4361 Avebury to Swindon road

The Head

Uffington Horse

The horse at Uffington is perhaps the best known and most loved of all the white horses.

It lies on the Berkshire Downs just over the Wiltshire border in the neighbouring county of Oxfordshire. The chalk hills that are so typical of Wiltshire do not stop at the county boundary and so a liberty has been taken to include this horse in this book. As the oldest surviving horse, around 3,000 years old, it is the forerunner for all the ones that followed, and its history shows the origins of this art form.

White Horse Hill faces north-west and falls down steeply into a dry valley known as the Manger. The stunning ripples of the hill were formed by melting snow during the last Ice Age. Below the horse at the bottom of the slope is

Location

OS grid reference: SU 302 866

2 miles (3km) south of Uffington village off B4507. On the Berkshire Downs below Iron Age hill fort called Uffington Castle overlooking the Vale of the White Horse.

Tour Directions

Distance 22½ miles (36km)

From the Hackpen horse continue over the hill to Marlborough and from there take the A346. Cross the M4 then on next roundabout turn right to Wanborough. Follow the B4507 to Ashbury. Turn right for the main car park and walk over the fields to get to the horse. There is a closer car park signposted for the elderly and disabled.

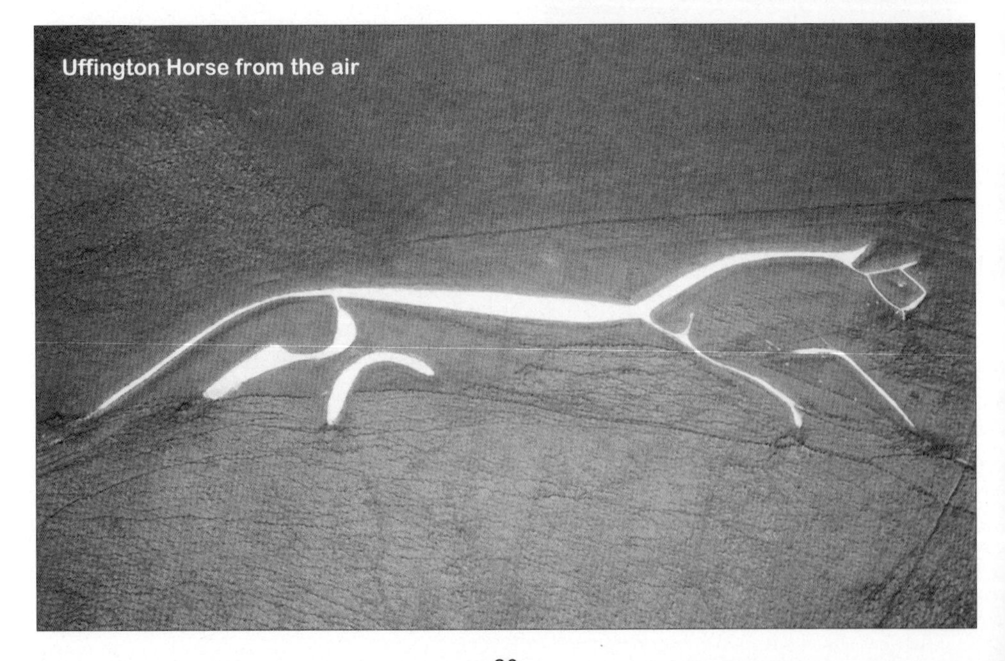

Uffington Horse from the air

The Manger from the horse's ear

a structure known as Dragon Hill. It is a natural chalk outcrop, which has been artificially levelled. Legend tells of how St George was supposed to have killed the dragon here and the patch where the grass never grows is where its blood was spilt.

The horse was not cut on the steepest part of the hill but on a lesser gradient nearer the brow below the early Iron Age hill fort of Uffington Castle. The position unfortunately makes it difficult to get a really good view from the ground.

In the 12th century it was recognised as being one of the 'Wonders of Britain'. It is quite a different stylised design to the other horses. During the eighteenth and nineteenth centuries it was fashionable to have horses that were considered true likenesses so this horse was was criticised for being rude and barbarous.

From as far back as medieval times it has been known as a horse yet some say it is not one at all but maybe a cat or dragon. The strangeness of the mouth certainly is not horse-like but as seen in the Bronze Age drawings and on the Iron Age coins art was more symbolic. In fact the similarities to these horses are quite striking. The earlier Bronze Age horses are long

Fact File

Cut around 3,000 years ago
Oldest surviving horse
Largest of all white horses
111 metres (365ft) nose to tail
Visible from 20 miles (32km)
Slope 30°
Best view is from B4508
4 miles (6½km) north of horse.

Dragon Hill from above the Horse

and flowing and the later Iron Age work, although more detailed, have beaky mouths and disjointed limbs.

Thank goodness that no one decided to remodel it in the same way as the Westbury horse. Its simple lines have huge appeal again these days and this may account for its increasing popularity. After all, we are often told that less is more.

Bronze Age Horse

Before the late Bronze Age date was accepted early antiquarians thought that it was made to commemorate King Alfred's victory over the Danes at Ashdown in 871.

Its origins were subject to speculation ever since until the introduction of Optical Stimulated Luminescence Dating. This is a technique, which tests the length of time that soil has been hidden from sunlight. The results were within a range of 1400-600 BC confirming that it was made at around the same time as Uffington Castle was becoming established. Perhaps it was a heraldic symbol.

Considering how often hill figures need to be maintained it is quite incredible that this one has survived so long. The secret of its success lies in a traditional festival that accompanied each scouring. No one knows the origin of the

'Pastime' as it was called, but it could go as far back as the horse itself. It is unlikely that the horse would still be here without it.

Roughly every seven years the people from across the Vale would undertake the heavy work of cleaning and renewing the chalk and were rewarded with refreshments and entertainment provided by the squire. Although by the 1700s the Pastime had grown into quite a bawdy occasion with sideshows, stalls, competitions and pickpockets. There were prizes offered for backsword play, grinning through a horse collar, racing downhill after cheeses and even for the woman who could smoke the most tobacco in an hour.

An old ballad sung by the villagers went:

'The owlde White Horse wants zettin to rights
And the Squire hav promised good cheer
Zo we'll gee un a scrape to kip un in zhape
And a'll last for many a year.

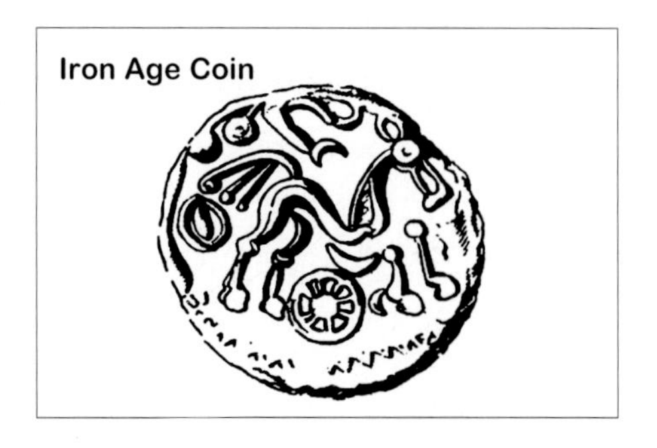
Iron Age Coin

Scouring today is much more low key and responsibility is taking jointly by English Heritage and the National Trust. They don't wait the traditional seven years to repair the horse but work on it whenever it is needed. It probably goes without saying that it is not accompanied by a ladies smoking competition!

Uffington Horse from the ground

Marlborough Horse

This is sometimes called the Preshute horse because it lies just above the village of Preshute.

Before Marlborough College was established there was a school in the High Street that was run by Mr Greasley. It was William Canning, one of his students, who designed this horse in 1804 and marked it out on the hill. His fellows helped him cut the outline and packed the cavity with chalk in the usual way. There seems to be no record of why they decided to do it but nevertheless its annual scouring became a much loved tradition of the school.

The design was basic with just two rather thick legs instead of the four elegant ones that are seen today.

After Mr Greasley's death around the time of 1830 there were

Location

OS grid reference: SU 184 682

1 mile (1½ km) south-west of Marlborough off A345. On Granham Hill overlooking Marlborough College and Preshute village.

Tour Directions

Distance 17 miles (27km)

From Uffington Horse retrace your path back to Marlborough along B4507 and then A346. Once there drive down the High Street then turn left at mini roundabout towards Pewsey.
Park near the Citroen garage and walk along the all weather footpath that follows the river or alternatively walk across the field to see the horse up close.

Marlborough Horse

The Head

no formal scourings and the horse was left to deteriorate. In 1873 Captain Reed, who also had been a schoolboy at the time and helped with the original cutting, was saddened by its neglect and organised its restoration. The legs were divided during the work and it still maintains this walking pose.

The last scouring before it was covered for the war was as part of the celebrations for King George V's silver jubilee in 1935.

Marlborough College is now responsible for the horse's well being. It is even mentioned in the school song but the pupils are no longer asked to do the work. The weeding and cleaning is done annually by groundsmen. The job probably doesn't take long as it is quite a small and slender horse. Years of chalk downshifting has built up the lower parts of the legs and belly making it look even thinner than was actually intended.

Until recently it was very difficult to see this horse but since the removal of certain trees the view has improved. It can be glimpsed from the A4 near the Marlborough College Memorial Hall but is best seen from the footpath that runs alongside the River Kennet immediately below the horse. If you climb to the top of the hill there is a great view of the College grounds.

Fact File

Cut in 1804
19 metres (62ft) nose to tail
14½ metres (48ft) ear to hoof
Visible for 2½ miles (4km)
Slope of 35°
Best view from footpath that runs below from A345 to Preshute House

Pewsey Horse

Pewsey Horse

This fairly recent horse was cut in 1937 to commemorate the coronation of King George VI. Like the Devizes horse it replaces an earlier one.

Robert Pile of Manor Farm, Alton Barnes, cut the old horse in 1785. He was the same man or possibly the father of the creator of the Alton Barnes horse, which was cut 27 years later.

It was reputed to have had a boy riding on its back but if it did there is now no trace of him.

Its first and only scouring took place in 1789 and in the tradition of the Uffington horse was accompanied by festival. The landowner objected to the poor behaviour at the festivities and would not give permission for the task to be repeated.

By the 1930s the horse was

Location

OS grid reference: SU 171 580

1½ miles (2½ km) south of Pewsey. On Pewsey Hill below the Everleigh road overlooking the Vale of Pewsey.

Tour Directions

Distance 8½ miles (13½ km)

From the Marlborough horse continue on the A345 towards Pewsey. Stay on A345 through the town then, after the garage on a sharp bend, turn left. The horse can be seen straight head. Follow the Everleigh road then park in a lay-by above the horse. Climb one of the stiles to gain access. Although the horse is fenced there is a gate that allows you to get a closer look.

completely overgrown. When George Marples was researching white horses for a book (subsequently written by his son, Morris) he found that he could just make out the outline of the head and body because the grass was a shade darker where the turf had once been disturbed.

While he was conducting his research a local committee who were looking for a suitable project to mark the coronation of the King approached him for his help. He was keen to assist and after rejecting the idea of re-establishing the old horse it was decided to create a new one.

Mr Marples designed the new one with the year 1937 marked out above the horse. As he had had difficulties in dating some of the other horses he decided that this would not be a problem for future researchers.

The Pewsey Fire Brigade were called in to do the job and the new horse now lies slightly above and to the left of the site of the old one. Throughout the week of the coronation the horse was lit by night as part of the celebrations.

Although the horse is scoured regularly the numbers of the year have since disappeared but as there are now plenty of written records the date of cutting will not be forgotten.

Fact File

Old horse cut in 1785

New horse cut in 1937

29½ metres (67ft) nose to tail

10½ metres (35ft) ear to hoof

Best view is from the A345 Salisbury road south of Pewsey.

The Head

Alton Barnes Horse

This horse is situated between Walkers Hill and Milk Hill, which is one of the highest points in Wiltshire and is part of the Pewsey Down Nature Reserve. On a clear day it is claimed that it can be seen from Old Sarum near Salisbury.

Its cutting was paid for by Robert Pile of Manor Farm - twice. He may have been the same Robert Pile who created the first Pewsey horse or he may have been his son as this was cut 27 years later in 1812.

He rather foolishly asked a travelling inn sign painter named John Thorne to design and cut the horse. He gave him £20 in advance and it was agreed that the horse would be excavated to a depth of ⅓ metre (1ft) and packed with chalk rubble.

Thorne went as far as providing

Location

OS grid reference: SU 106 637

1 mile (1½ km) north of the village Alton Barnes. It lies on an escarpment between Walkers Hill and Milk Hill near the long barrow called Adam's Grave.Overlooks the Vale of Pewsey.

Tour Directions

Distance 6½ miles (10½ km)

Retrace your path back into Pewsey and take a left turn to Alton Barnes. Once there take the Devizes road to get a good view, or if you want to visit the horse turn right up the hill and park in one of the lay-bys . It is a fairly long walk across the nature reserve but well worth it on a good day.

Alton Barnes Horse

The Head

a sketch of the horse, which resembled the walking pose of the horse at Cherhill but with ears that were only outlined in chalk. The sketch was made from the canal bridge at Honey Street (this is still a good place to view the horse). Instead of doing the hard work himself he employed a local man to do the digging giving him the opportunity to disappear with the money.

He was later caught and found guilty of a series of crimes for which he was hanged.

Mr Pile had to then pay again to finally see his project finished.

At times this horse has fallen into disrepair but it has always had just enough attention to keep it from disappearing altogether. A scouring in 1866 used fresh chalk that was dug from a pit near the horse's head presumably to save the time and effort of carting it from further afield. This was a mistake as the pit never really grew over again properly and can still be seen quite clearly.

A more recent scouring in 1987 used chalk that was flown in with the help of army helicopters.

A fence to prevent damage from the feet of careless visitors and livestock frames the horse, but unfortunately it has little effect on the rabbits that continue to undermine it.

Fact File

Cut in 1812
49 metres (160ft) nose to tail
55 metres (180ft) ear to hoof
Visible for 22 miles (35½ km)
35° slope
Best view from the canal bridge at Honey Street

Roundway Hill - site of the old Devizes Horse, now completely grown over

Lost Wiltshire Horses

As has been seen throughout this book regular maintenance is vital to their survival and not all have been fortunate enough to receive the care they deserve.

Some have been replaced. The old Westbury horse was deliberately covered by the new one while others, such as Pewsey and Devizes, had disappeared many years before the new horses were designed as tributes to them.

At Tan Hill there was once a horse that was known as the Tan Hill Donkey because it had a rather large head. It was last seen in 1975 and then it was only partially visible. The legs were very overgrown but it would have been a similar size to the horse at Broad Town. Situated on the western face of the hill it overlooked a small stone circle and there was a path from it that led up the hill. The stone circle now lies in ruins and the horse has completely disappeared.

There were others, probably even more than we know about. In 1948 a previously unknown horse unexpectedly came to light at Rockley. A field was ploughed and it was noticed that a large amount of chalk rubble was exposed. An aerial photo showed it had the recognisable outline of a trotting horse.

Positioned on a slight slope, 4 miles (6.5km) north west of Marlborough, near the top of the hill it would have been best seen from the old Marlborough to Swindon road that only survives today as a track. No attempt was made to save the horse and it has since disappeared without trace.

Other Wiltshire Hill Figures

All the other hill carvings that lie in Wiltshire were made after 1900. Most were cut during or soon after the First World War by soldiers stationed in the area.

The most striking are a set of military badges worked into the hillsides at Fovant. There were up to twenty badges here at one time, each regiment would try and outdo the others with bigger and better efforts. Because of the intricate designs several have been lost. Twelve remain and are maintained by the charity The Fovant Badges Society to ensure that these too do not fall into disrepair.

One of the designs, the Badge of the Australian Commonwealth Military Forces, also appears on a hillside at Codford. It was cut by the Australian troops who were stationed there.

Soldiers also cut the Kiwi at Bulford. They were the New Zealand Canterbury Engineers but this was not a voluntary exercise. The troops were ordered to create this hill figure to keep them from going on the rampage while they were waiting to return home after the war had ended. It is a well thought out design that was altered to counter the foreshortening effect. Like some other chalk carvings it was used for advertising - this time for Kiwi shoe polish.

Last but not least there is the panda at Laverstock. This is a much later creation. Cut in 1969 by undergraduates it was done in only one night as a rag week prank. Apparently the symbol for that year was the panda. Despite the police being called the panda remained and was even recut the following year.

Badge of the Wiltshire Regiment at Fovant

Other British Hill Figures

There are plenty of areas of chalk in Britain but hill carving never really caught on elsewhere like it did in Wiltshire.

There are some however. Most of them are either white crosses or giants, and as with all of the older figures they are notoriously difficult to date.

The white crosses, it is argued, cannot be older than Christianity as they are plainly a Christian symbol. There are two within four miles (6½ km) of each other in Buckinghamshire. The Whiteleaf Cross is the largest. It sits on a triangular base 122 metres (400ft) wide which the locals call the globe. It may date to Roman times, as there are images on Roman coins that show similar crosses on top of tapered plinths. Or it may be of later origin and the base was the result of many years of chalk down-washing that was eventually incorporated into the shape. Of the giants there are only two still visible and these also have mysterious origins. The Long Man of Wilmington in Sussex is the largest British giant. He stands in outline on the hill with a stave in each hand. His old chalk trenches 80cm (32ins) wide have grassed over, and since 1874 he has been depicted in pale yellow bricks. His image before this would have been much bolder.

The other giant is in Dorset and is probably the most famous. The Cerne Abbas Giant is naked apart from a belt or girdle and holds a club above his head. His obvious arousal causes either embarrassment or amusement to most people. The naked stance was usual for an Iron Age man about to do battle, and this, as well as the abundance of Iron Age remains in the area, has led many to think he originated at that time.

Cerne Abbas Giant